God Gave Your Soul Eternal Worth

JENNI GUZMAN BAUTISTA

Olympus Story House

Hush little baby don't say a word,
God gave your soul eternal worth.
And if you ever doubt His grace,
Promise you'll seek His holy face.

Hush little baby don't say a word,
God gave to us both heaven and earth.
And in His image He made you,
Fear not my love for His word is true.

Hush little baby don't say a word,
God made the rocks and trees and birds.
Then came a soul that He already knew,
And He made me a mom special just for you.

Hush little baby don't say a word,
Each day is a gift that we don't deserve.
There is an order in all you see and hear,
A plan and a purpose for you, my dear.

Hush little baby don't say a word,
In the quiet of your soul His voice is heard.
Peace can be found in every heart,
And yours, my child, is a work of art.

Hush little baby don't say a word,
You had His blessing long before your birth.
And when you raise His name in prayer,
He'll welcome you to His arms with care.

Hush little baby don't say a word,
There will be hard things that you endure.
So let us embrace these moments here,
And know you can trust Him with your tears.

Hush little baby don't say a word,
God clears a path that once was blurred.
Remember to be grateful
for the smallest things,
For in the midst of falling,
He'll give you wings.

Hush little baby don't say a word,
His promise of salvation we are assured.
And as you grow, love, I'll do what's right,
Showing you a faith in eternal life.

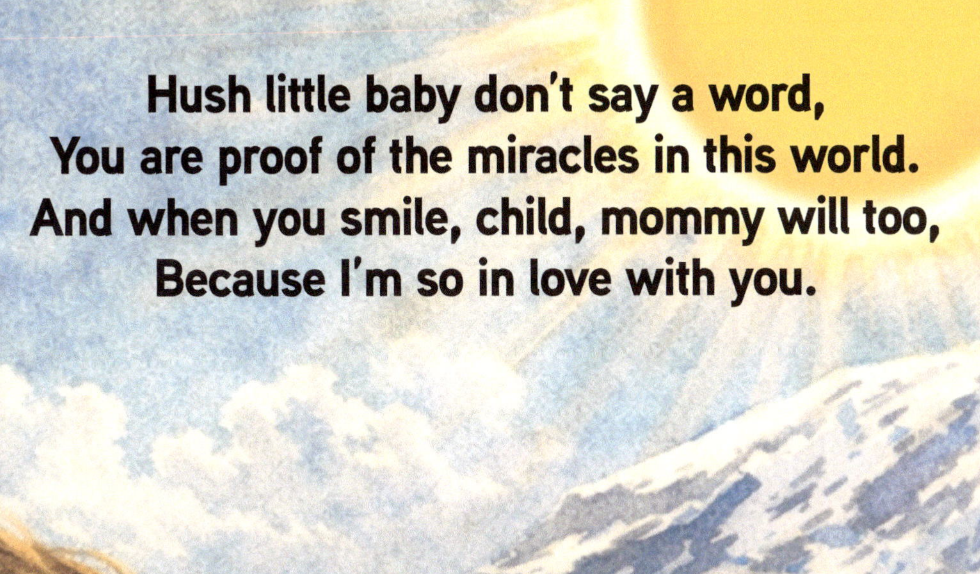

Hush little baby don't say a word,
You are proof of the miracles in this world.
And when you smile, child, mommy will too,
Because I'm so in love with you.

9 781969 422911